That's not my...
sticker book
Farm

This book belongs to...

_____

That's not my hen.

That's my — — .

3

That's not my dog.

That's my _ _ _ _.

That's not my cow.

That's my — — —.

That's not my duck.

That's my _ _ _ _

That's not my pig.

That's my — — — .

That's not my goat.

Hen
pages 2-3

Dog
pages 4-5

Cow pages 6-7

Duck pages 8-9

Pig
pages 10–11

Goat
pages
12–13

Farmhouse
pages 14–15

Sheep pages 16–17

Tractor pages 18–19

Donkey pages 20–21

Scarecrow
pages 22-23

Field
page 24

That's my _ _ _ _ _.

That's not my farmhouse.

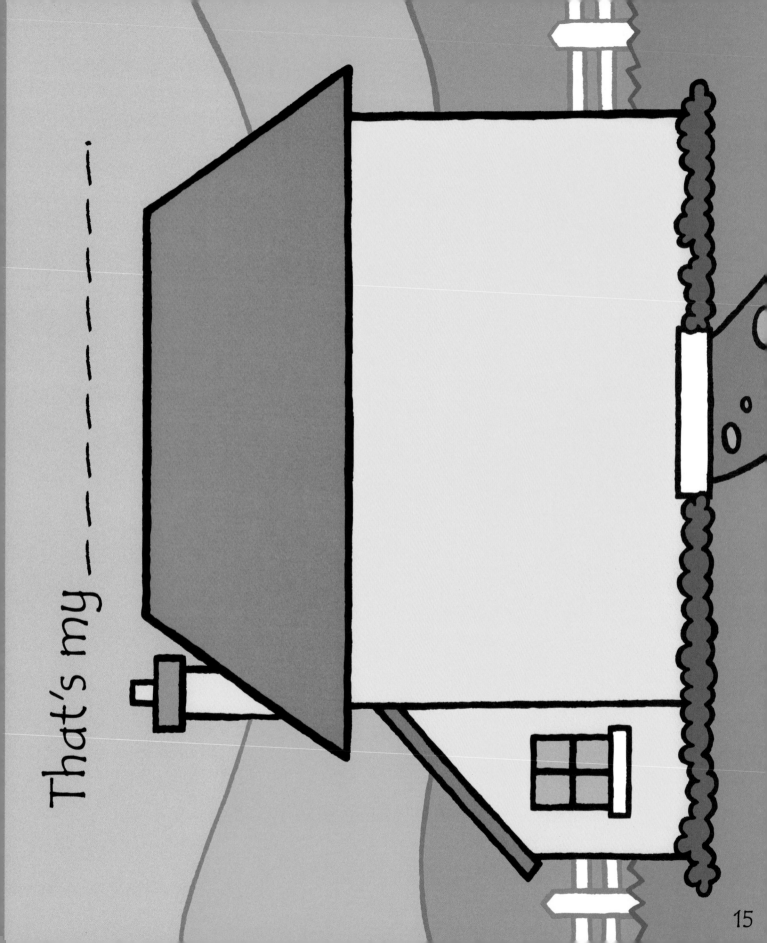

That's my _ _ _ _ _ _ _ .

15

That's not my sheep.

That's my _ _ _ _ _ _ _.

17

That's not my tractor.

That's my — — — — —.

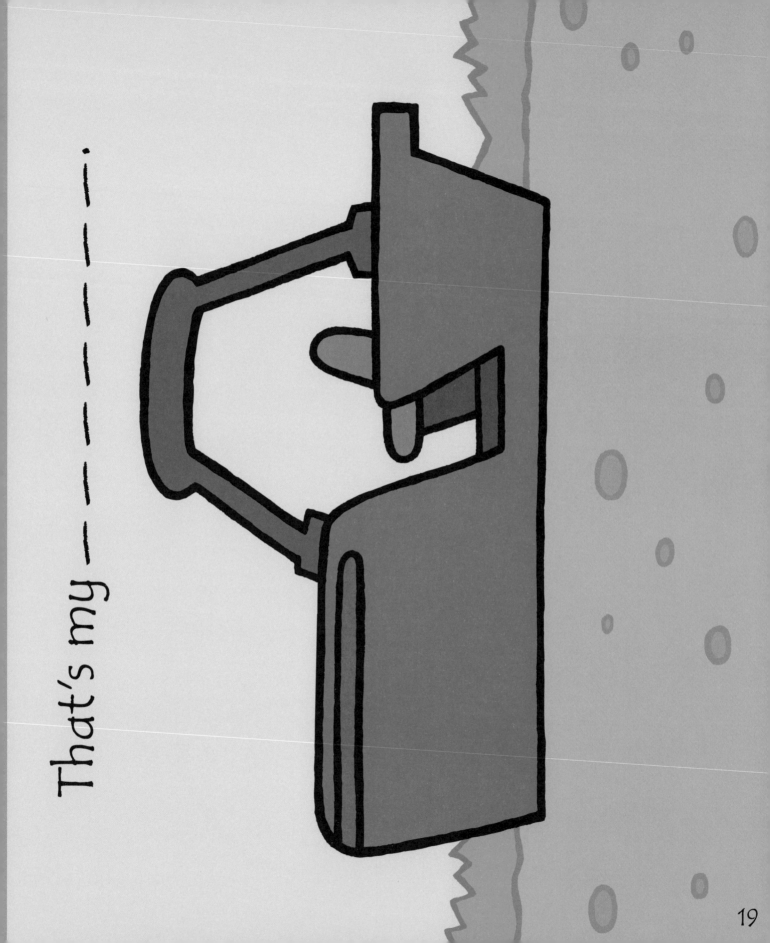

That's not my donkey.

That's my _____.

That's not my scarecrow.

That's my _ _ _ _ _ _ _ _ _ _ _ _ _.

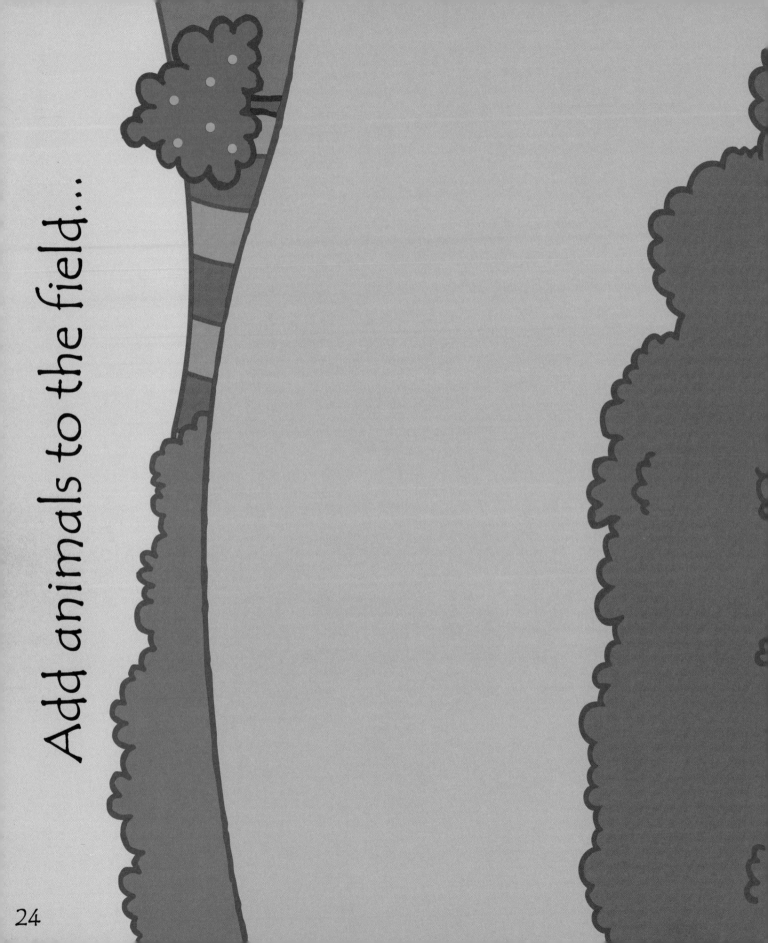

Add animals to the field....